Copyrig

Sword of the I

ISBN 978-0-

All Scripture quotations are from
the King James Bible.

Printed and Bound in the United States of America

Heaven

Bible Answers to Questions Most Often Asked About Heaven

"Let not your heart be troubled: ye believe in God, believe also in me. In my Father's house are many mansions: if it were not so, I would have told you. I go to prepare a place for you. And if I go and prepare a place for you, I will come again, and receive you unto myself; that where I am, there ye may be also."—John 14:1–3.

When I was a small boy I heard the preacher talk about Heaven. He said when the Christian dies he goes up to Heaven. I used to lie on my bed at night, and wonder: *Is Heaven a real place? If Heaven is a real place, where is it? If I were to die as a Christian, would I go to Heaven immediately? If I did, how long would it take me to make the trip? And when I got to Heaven, would I know my friends? Would they know me? What would I look like in Heaven? Would I have a body? Could I eat in Heaven? Would my loved ones know me?*

Would I know my loved ones? Would I know my grandmother and grandfather who had already gone to Heaven? These and many other questions went through my mind—death and Heaven were mysteries to me.

One of the greatest causes of sorrow, when our loved ones pass away, is a lack of knowledge concerning the dead. The Bible says in I Thessalonians 4:13, "I would not have you to be ignorant, brethren, concerning them which are asleep, that ye sorrow not, even as others which have no hope." Here is a suggestion that a lack of knowledge is the chief cause of sorrow when we lose our loved ones.

I will try to answer several questions about Heaven.

1. Is Heaven a Real Place?

Yes, the Bible teaches that Heaven is a real, literal, physical place. Jesus said in John 14:2 and 3,

> "I go to prepare a place for you. And if I go and prepare a place for you, I will come again, and receive you unto myself; that where I am, there ye may be also."

I mention that Heaven is a place because some think that Heaven is a state of the mind. Jesus said:

> "Lay not up for yourselves treasures upon earth, where moth and rust doth corrupt, and where thieves break through and steal: But lay up for yourselves treasures in heaven, where neither moth nor rust doth corrupt, and where

thieves do not break through nor steal"—
Matt. 6:19, 20.

Now, friends, that could only be said of an actual, real, literal, physical place.

If I had time to read Revelation 21 and 22 you would see a beautiful description of the Holy City, the New Jerusalem, which is the eternal home of the saved. In those chapters the Bible says that Heaven has foundations, and the foundations are garnished with all manner of precious stones. The Bible says the walls of the city are made of jasper. It goes on to say that there are three gates on the east, three on the west, three on the north, three on the south, and it says the gates are made of pearl and every several gate is of one pearl.

Say, that could not be said of a state of mind; it could only be said of a real, literal place.

In Revelation 21 and 22, the Bible gives the measurements of the Holy City. It is given in cubits. If you were to take the cubits and multiply them into feet and then divide them into miles, you would find that the Holy City, the New Jerusalem, is fifteen hundred miles square—fifteen hundred miles in four different directions!

Now, friends, there is no way to measure the state of a man's mind. You could not measure Heaven unless it was a real, literal, physical place.

2. What Kind of Place Is Heaven?

First, Heaven is a place of indescribable beauty and glory. The Bible says in I Corinthians 2:9, "Eye hath not seen, nor ear heard, neither have entered into the heart of man [or crossed man's mind], the things which God hath prepared for them that love him."

Wait a minute. The Bible says it has never crossed man's mind; there is no way to imagine the indescribable beauty of Heaven! I suggest you read Revelation 21 and 22, and when you finish, you will have only a little glimpse of the beautiful place called Heaven.

One night a young boy was walking with his grandfather. It was a beautiful night. The sky was brilliantly lit with a million stars on parade. The little boy pulled at his grandfather's coattail and said, "Grandpa, Grandpa, if Heaven is so beautiful on the outside, what must the inside look like!"

The songwriter was correct when she wrote:

> How beautiful Heaven must be,
> Sweet home of the happy and free.

Heaven is a place of indescribable beauty and glory.

But Heaven, too, is a place of perfect rest. The Bible says in Revelation 14:13, "Blessed are the dead which die in the Lord from henceforth: Yea, saith the Spirit, that they may rest from their labours; and their works do follow them."

Most people here never know what it is to

experience complete and perfect rest, with no worries, no schedules to meet, no time clocks to punch, and no alarm clocks to awake you early in the morning.

When my mother died I was on soul-winning visitation. Some friends found me and told me that Mother had passed away. Hurrying home I entered the bedroom where Mother had been for several weeks due to illness. And there on the bed lay my mother's body. When I looked at her my first impression was, "Mother, this is the first time in my life I've ever seen you relaxed." She always had a burden of some kind to carry; now she was resting from her labors. The burdens were gone.

Heaven is a place of indescribable beauty. It is a place of perfect rest. But Heaven, too, is a place of open vision.

There are so many things I cannot explain here.

I remember a young couple with three small children. I was called to conduct the funeral of one of those little children. A few months later the second child died. And in less than a year the third child died. They had unrelated diseases. It was an unusual thing, and I had never had an experience like it. As we walked away from the grave of their last child the mother wept and said, "Explain to me why this happened; why did God take every child we had while other families never lose a child?"

Friends, I could not explain it, because I cannot see the end from the beginning. But God knows.

Romans 8:28 is true. It is the Word of God. It is a fact. "All things [DO] work together for good to them that love God."

I said to that young couple, "You may not always be able to trace God, but you can always trust Him."

> My Father's way may twist and turn,
>   My heart may throb and ache;
> But in my soul, I'm glad I know
>   He maketh no mistake.

God knows what He is doing. I cannot explain everything now. I cannot see as God sees. But in Heaven I'll know. Heaven is a place of open vision, with no glass between and there I will understand it all. First Corinthians 13:12 says, "Now we see through a glass, darkly; but then face to face: now I know in part; but then shall I know even as also I am known."

I read the story of a young boy in England who, due to his father's death, had to drop out of school and go to work to make a living for his family. He was only ten or eleven years old. He sold papers to help his mother provide for other family members.

Each day after selling his papers, he stopped at a toy store on his way home to look at some beautifully painted toy soldiers in the window. The storekeeper had noticed this.

Then one day he missed the boy. He inquired of those in the street, "Has anyone seen the little paper boy who used to stop and look at the toy soldiers?"

Someone said, "Oh, haven't you heard? He was hit

by an automobile the other day, and he is in the hospital unconscious."

The storekeeper was moved: he gathered up the little toy soldiers and took them to the hospital. He told the boy's mother how the boy had looked wishfully at the soldiers every day and then he asked permission to give them to him. The boy was unconscious, so the man placed the beautiful, little soldiers across the foot of the bed. They stayed there several days.

One morning when the boy regained consciousness, the first thing he saw was the toy soldiers. He could hardly believe his eyes. He began moving forward. Reaching with his little hands to touch the soldiers, getting closer and closer, until finally the soldiers were in his hands. With a smile he exclaimed, "Oh, look, Mother! Look! Here are the soldiers, and there is no glass between!"

3. Do the Saved Go to Heaven Immediately?

The answer is yes. The Bible says in II Corinthians 5:8, "to be absent from the body" is "to be present with the Lord."

There are only two places a Christian can ever be: in the body or with the Lord.

In Philippians 1:23 Paul said, "I am in a strait betwixt two, having a desire to depart, and to be with

Christ; which is far better." Depart and be with Christ. Man is not a body; man is a soul. He has a body. The Bible says that God created man in His own image, and that God breathed into his nostrils and he became a living soul (Gen. 2:7). My body is not me. It is mine. My body is my possession. If I bump my head, I say, "I bumped my head." It is my head, my hands, my feet, my ears, etc. But it is also my watch and my coat. My coat is my possession and my body is my possession. The body is simply the house in which I live. I am the soul and spirit on the inside. In I Thessalonians 5:23 Paul said, "I pray God your whole spirit and soul and body be preserved blameless unto the coming of our Lord Jesus Christ." When a man dies, his soul and spirit leave his body and go immediately to be with Christ.

In London, England, a tombstone has an unusual epitaph. A man named Solomon Peas gave instruction before he died to put these words on his tombstone:

> Beneath these clouds and beneath these trees,
> Lies the body of Solomon Peas;
> This is not Peas; it is only his pod;
> Peas has shelled out and gone Home to God.

When I read that, I wished my name were Solomon Peas; I would like to have that on my tombstone.

When the Christian dies, he goes immediately to be with Christ: absent from the body; present with the Lord.

4. Will We Know Each Other in Heaven?

The Bible indicates we will. Jesus said, "...when ye shall see Abraham, and Isaac, and Jacob, and all the prophets, in the kingdom of God." Here the Bible teaches that we will know Abraham, Isaac and Jacob.

On the Mount of Transfiguration, Moses and Elijah appeared with Christ. Now, keep in mind that Moses lived and died long before Elijah was born. But on the Mount of Transfiguration Moses knew Elijah, and Elijah knew Moses. They not only knew each other but they still had the same names.

Someone asks, "Will we have our same name in Heaven?" I don't know. I know Moses was still Moses, and Elijah was still Elijah, Abraham was still Abraham, Isaac was still Isaac, and Jacob was still Jacob. Maybe we will.

Will we know each other in Heaven? Yes. Moses knew Elijah, and Elijah knew Moses, though they had never met on earth. They not only knew each other, but they knew what would happen in the future. And the Bible says in Luke 9 that they discussed the death that Jesus should accomplish in Jerusalem. First Corinthians 13:12: "Now we see through a glass, darkly; but then face to face: now I know in part; but then shall I know even as also I am known."

Yes, dear friends, I will know my mother in Heaven. I will know my dear grandfather who died when I was a little boy. I will know my grandmother who lived to be ninety-nine years of age.

5. Will We Have a Body in Heaven?

The Bible seems to indicate that we will. In Luke 16, when Lazarus died and was carried by angels to Abraham's bosom, the rich man looked across a great gulf and saw Lazarus in Abraham's bosom. And in the conversation with Abraham he asked that Lazarus dip his finger in water. That implies that Lazarus had a body.

In II Corinthians 5:1 Paul says, "For we know that if our earthly house of this tabernacle were dissolved, we have a building of God, an house not made with hands, eternal in the heavens." He goes on to say that in this tabernacle we groan, desiring to be clothed upon with our body or tabernacle which is from Heaven.

The Bible does indicate that there will be a body between death and resurrection. It is a body that will be occupied until Jesus comes and this body is raised.

Friends, the Bible teaches that Jesus is coming. When He comes, the bodies of Christians will be raised from the dead. First Thessalonians 4:16 says, "The Lord himself shall descend from heaven with a shout, with the voice of the archangel, and with the trump of God: and the dead in Christ shall rise first." Christians are going to come out of the graves.

The Bible says in Acts 24:15, "There shall be a

resurrection of the dead, both of the just and unjust."

In John 5:28, 29 Jesus said,

> "Marvel not at this: for the hour is coming, in the which all that are in the graves shall hear his voice, And shall come forth; they that have done good, unto the resurrection of life; and they that have done evil, unto the resurrection of damnation."

In Job 19:25–27 Job said,

> "I know that my redeemer liveth, and that he shall stand at the latter day upon the earth: And though after my skin worms destroy this body, yet in my flesh shall I see God: Whom I shall see for myself, and mine eyes shall behold, and not another."

The Bible teaches that when a man dies, his soul and spirit leave the body and go immediately to be with Christ. And based on II Corinthians 5, that soul and spirit occupy a temporary body between death and resurrection while awaiting the resurrection of this body. So I suppose the body of II Corinthians 5 is a temporary body that the believer occupies, between death and resurrection; but when Jesus comes, the Bible says, the dead in Christ shall be raised first. And when this body is raised, the Bible teaches that it will be a body exactly like Jesus'.

> "Beloved, now are we the sons of God, and it doth not yet appear what we shall be: but we know that, when he shall appear, we shall be like him; for we shall see him as he is."—I John 3:2.

"For our conversation [or citizenship] is in heaven; from whence also we look for the Saviour, the Lord Jesus Christ: Who shall change our vile body, that it may be fashioned like unto his glorious body."—Phil. 3:20, 21.

Now here is the picture: the Christian dies; his soul and spirit leave his body and go immediately to be with Christ. His body is buried. The body goes back to dust. It may be a hundred years before Jesus comes. It may be a thousand years. On the other hand, it may be only a year or maybe a day. Nobody knows when.

But when Jesus comes, the Bible says He will come with a shout, with the voice of the archangel and with the trump of God and the dead in Christ shall be raised first. The body of that Christian will be raised from the dead. The soul and spirit that have been with Christ since death will be brought back.

"But I would not have you to be ignorant, brethren, concerning them which are asleep, that ye sorrow not, even as others which have no hope. For if we believe that Jesus died and rose again, even so them also which sleep in Jesus will God bring with him."—I Thess. 4:13, 14.

When Jesus comes, the saints who have died will come back with Him. The body will be raised and the soul and spirit will be reunited with the resurrection body and in eternity the person will be with Christ.

First Thessalonians 4:17 says, "And so shall we ever be with the Lord."

Now I raise the question,

6. Do the Saved in Heaven Know What Is Happening on Earth?

The answer is yes, as I will show you from a number of Bible verses. The saved in Heaven are conscious and awake. Some think that when a man dies he goes to sleep and knows nothing until the resurrection. The Bible does say that man sleeps, but "sleep" has reference only to the body.

First Thessalonians 4:13: "I would not have you to be ignorant, brethren, concerning them which are asleep." In John 11, Jesus spoke of Lazarus as being asleep. But that has no reference to the soul and spirit. There are other Bible verses that teach that those in Heaven are conscious and know what is happening on earth.

Here is a good rule to follow when interpreting the Bible: never use an obscure passage to contradict a clear one.

Let me show you several verses that teach that those in Heaven are conscious and awake.

Luke 15:7 and 10 say there is more rejoicing in Heaven over one sinner who repents than over ninety-nine just persons who need no repentance. The rejoicing is not by the angels, because angels do not know what salvation is. The only ones who can rejoice are those who know about salvation.

Up in Heaven, the saved look down on earth. They see friends and loved ones who accept Christ as Saviour, and they rejoice over their salvation.

We read in Revelation 6:9 and 10 when the fifth seal was opened,

> *"I saw under the altar the souls of them that were slain for the word of God, and for the testimony which they held: And they cried with a loud voice, saying, How long, O Lord, holy and true, dost thou not judge and avenge our blood on them that dwell on the earth?"*

Now, these people in Heaven are those who had been martyred or slain. The Bible says they cried out with a loud voice. They were not asleep. Rather, they were talking to the Lord and asking Him how long before He did something about those who had martyred them.

Notice several things here. These people in Heaven could look back on earth, and they saw the people who had martyred them were getting by without punishment. So they asked the Lord, "How long...dost thou not judge and avenge our blood on them that dwell on the earth?"

Notice something else. The Lord spoke back to them, and verse 11 says, "And white robes were given unto every one of them; and it was said unto them, that they should rest yet for a little season, until their fellowservants also and their brethren, that should be killed as they were, should be fulfilled."

Now do the saved in Heaven know what is happening on earth?

Hebrews 12:1: "Wherefore seeing we also are compassed about with so great a cloud of witnesses..." These witnesses are those mentioned in Hebrews 11, which lists at least seventeen names: then Hebrews 12 begins, "Wherefore seeing we also are compassed about with so great a cloud of witnesses..."

In the original manuscripts, there were no chapter-and-verse divisions. These were added by men. Spurgeon complained about those who chopped the Bible up into chapters and verses. I think his complaint is justified. Now if we stop at the end of Hebrews 11, we miss a very important truth, because Hebrews 12:1 teaches that those in Heaven know what is happening on earth. We are "compassed about" with such a great cloud of witnesses.

Do the saved in Heaven know what is happening on earth? Yes. How much do they know? I am not sure they see all the sin and sorrow. I am not sure they see all the murder and wickedness. But I do know they know when unsaved people trust Christ as Saviour, because Luke 15:10 says they rejoice in the presence of the angels of God over one sinner who repents.

Man's existence is divided into three stages—the present, the intermediate and the eternal. The present is from the time a man is born until he dies. The intermediate is from the time a man dies until he is resurrected. And the eternal is from the time a man is resurrected on through eternity. I say through because it is a common expression. Of course, there is no such thing as going through eternity. When a man is resurrected, from that point on is the eternal state.

I am living in the present. If I were to die right now, my soul and spirit would leave my body and go to be with Christ. My body would be buried. And that intermediate stage would be the time between death and resurrection, while we await the coming of Christ.

There are several theories concerning this intermediate time. Some say there is soul-sleep, that people don't know what is happening. Our dear Catholic friends say there is a purgatory where unconfessed sins are purged before going on to Heaven. But the Bible says that between death and resurrection a man is with Christ, that he is conscious, that he has a body, and that he does know what is happening on earth.

Now there is another question I want to ask regarding Heaven:

7. Where Is Heaven?

When I was a little boy, I used to say "up to Heaven." When I got older, someone reminded me that if I died in China and went up I would be going an opposite direction from a man who died in America and went up. Since the world is round and China is on the other side of the world, that seems reasonable. But I have discovered from the Bible that Heaven is in a fixed location in the sides of the North beyond the highest star.

Here is an interesting passage: "Promotion cometh neither from the **east**, nor from the **west**, nor from the **south**. But God is the judge: he putteth down one, and setteth up another" (Ps. 75:6,7).

Isn't it strange that the word "north" is left out? Why? Because promotion does come from the North. It comes from God. "He putteth down one, and setteth up another."

In Isaiah 14:12—17 we have the story of Lucifer, who became Satan. He said, "I will exalt my throne above the stars of God." He said, "I will ascend above the heights of the clouds." He said, "I will sit...in the sides of the north."

Heaven, then, is in a fixed location in the sides of the North. According to Isaiah 14, it is beyond the highest star.

Here in Isaiah 14 Satan said, "I will ascend into heaven, I will exalt my throne above the stars of God." If he is talking about literal stars, he is talking about going out beyond what we call the second heaven.

There are three heavens. Paul said in II Corinthians 12:2 and 4,

> "I knew a man in Christ above fourteen years ago, (whether in the body, I cannot tell; or whether out of the body, I cannot tell: God knoweth;) such an one caught up to the third heaven....How that he was caught up into

19

paradise, and heard unspeakable words, which it is not lawful for a man to utter."

If there is a third Heaven, there is a second and first heaven. The first heaven is the atmospheric heavens where the birds fly. Says II Peter 3:10, "The heavens shall pass away with a great noise." He is speaking of the atmospheric heavens. Psalm 19:1 says, "The heavens declare the glory of God." This is talking about the second heaven—the starry or planetary heavens. And the third Heaven, the Paradise of God, where Christians go and where Jesus is, is somewhere out beyond the last star, beyond the second or starry heaven.

I am told that the farthest star man has been able to locate through his most powerful telescopes is 500 million light years away. Light travels a little more than 186,000 miles per second. That means if you could go 186,000 miles per second, it would take 500 million years to reach the last star that man has been able to locate, and Heaven is somewhere out beyond the highest star, "in the sides of the north," according to Isaiah 14.

So when I said, "Up to Heaven," as a little boy, I was right, though I did not understand it. Any time you go North you are going up. Everybody says "up North" and "down South." And the North Pole is the top of the earth. So Heaven is up.

Heaven is real. It is in a fixed location "in the sides of the north," beyond the highest star.

8. Who Is Going to Heaven?

Suppose I ask you, Who is going to Heaven? Some would say the man who reads his Bible and prays. Others would say the man who lives good and keeps the Ten Commandments. Still others would say the man who attends church faithfully or the man who has been baptized. I have even heard people say if a man suffers enough here he goes to Heaven when he dies.

When I was a small boy, there was a great fire in Atlanta, Georgia. The Winecoff Hotel burned and many people lost their lives. Someone wrote a song (it was supposed to have been a gospel song) about the Winecoff Fire. One verse of the song went like this:

> Surely there's a Heaven
> For folks who die this way;
> And we'll go Home to see them
> In Heaven some sweet day.

The implication is, since they suffered in a fire, they would go to Heaven. Yes, people have different ideas about how to go to Heaven.

When I worked at the Post Office, a lady came in and said, "Preacher, the way I see this business about Heaven is: we are all at the Post Office this morning. You came up Covington Highway and out Candler Road and you are here. So-and-So came through Panthersville, and he is here. I came through East Lake Park and I am here."

She went on to describe how a number of people had all arrived at the Post Office, none having come the same way. When she finished, she said, "Now that is the way it is about Heaven. We are all working for the same thing and as long as we are sincere we will all go to Heaven when we die." Then she asked, "What do you think about that?"

I replied, "There is only one thing wrong with it: when we die, we are not going to the Post Office."

There are many ways to the Post Office, but only one way to Heaven. John 14:6: "I am **the** way, **the** truth, and **the** life: no man cometh unto the Father, but by me." Acts 4:12: "Neither is there salvation in any other: for there is none other name under heaven given among men, whereby we must be saved."

Now, who is going to Heaven? Let's see what the Bible says. In Revelation 7 we have a heavenly scene. There is an innumerable host, clothed in white robes. Revelation 7:13 says, "And one of the elders answered, saying unto me, What are these which are arrayed in white robes? and whence came they?"

Now, notice the question of one of the elders: "How did these people get here? From whence came they?" John answered in verse 14, "Sir, thou knowest. And he said to me, These are they which came out of great tribulation, and have washed their robes, and made them white in the blood of the Lamb." These people in Heaven were there because they had washed their robes and made them white in the blood of the Lamb.

Friends, only those who have been washed in the blood are going to Heaven.

But what does it mean to be washed in the blood? There is no way we can take the blood of Jesus and put it into a basin and wash our hands. We have never seen that blood. Let me briefly explain.

The Bible teaches that all men are sinners. "For all have sinned, and come short of the glory of God" (Rom. 3:23). The Bible says in verse 10, "As it is written, There is none righteous, no, not one." Not all men have committed the same sins or the same number of sins, but all have sinned. Since all men are sinners, all men owe a penalty. Sin demands a price. Ezekiel 18:4: "The soul that sinneth, it shall die." Romans 6:23: "The wages of sin is death." James 1:15: "Sin, when it is finished, bringeth forth death."

Now, here is the picture: I am a sinner. I have sinned. And being a sinner I owe a penalty. The penalty for sin is death. But that death is more than dying with a gunshot wound or cancer. That death is described in the Bible as the second death, the lake of fire. Revelation 20:14: "Death and hell were cast into the lake of fire. This is the second death." If I pay what I owe as a sinner, I must go into Hell and stay there forever and ever and ever.

Now, here is the bright side of the story. The Bible teaches that two thousand years ago God took every sin I ever have committed and all I ever will commit and placed those sins on Jesus. That is not just preacher talk but exactly what the Bible says in Isaiah 53:6: "The LORD hath laid on him the iniquity of us all." Two thousand years ago God looked down through the telescope of time and saw every sin that I ever would commit, and He took those sins—one by one—and placed them over on Jesus. And I Peter 2:24 says, "Who his own self bare our sins in his own body on the tree." The Bible also says in II Corinthians 5:21, "He hath made him to be sin for us, who knew no sin; that we might be made the righteousness of God in him."

Now, you can never change the fact that two thousand years ago God took every sin you have ever committed, all you ever will commit, if you live to be a thousand years old, and placed those sins on Jesus; and while Jesus was bearing our sins in His own body, God actually punished Him in our place to pay the debt we owe.

Someone said the Jews killed Him. But that is not so. Others say the Roman soldiers killed Him. They are wrong. The Bible says, "For God so loved the world, that he gave his only begotten Son." And Romans 8:32 says, "He...spared not his own Son, but delivered him up for us all." God actually punished Jesus in our place to pay the debt we owe so that when we die we won't have to pay it.

That sounds like everyone is saved, doesn't it? It sounds like everyone will go to Heaven, because He died for everyone. But everyone is not saved. The

24

death of Jesus Christ on the cross is sufficient for all, but it is efficient only to those who believe.

Here is what happened. God transferred your sins to Christ, and on the cross Jesus Christ died for you. He shed His blood. Leviticus 17:11 tells us, "The life of the flesh is in the blood." Blood in the body means the man is alive. Shed blood speaks of death. When Jesus shed His blood, He gave His life for you. He paid what you and I owe. He suffered what we should have suffered.

That is what we mean when we sing:

> What can wash away my sin?
> Nothing but the blood of Jesus.

Hebrews 9:22 says, "Without shedding of blood is no remission." When Jesus died in our place, He shed His blood. That is what it means when it says they "have washed their robes, and made them white in the blood of the Lamb." It means they believe that Jesus Christ died for them, that He suffered their death and paid their debt and they are trusting Him as Saviour.

Now let me briefly sum up what I have said. We are sinners. We owe the sin debt. God transferred our guilt to Jesus. Jesus shed His blood. He died on a cross. He paid what we owe. That is what He meant when He cried out from the cross, "It is finished." Now for us to be washed in the blood, or to accept the payment, we must do it by faith. John 3:16 says, "For God so loved the world, that he gave his only begotten Son, that whosoever believeth in him should not

25

perish, but have everlasting life."

The main hang-up is over that little word "believe." Everybody says, "I have always believed in Christ. I'm not an atheist." But the Bible word "believe" does not mean to accept the historical fact that He was a Person who lived and died. To "believe" means to trust, to depend, to rely on.

I have often illustrated faith by an airplane.

We go to the airport. You say to me, "Is that a plane?"

"Yes."

"Do you believe the plane will fly?"

"Yes."

"Do you believe the plane will take you to California?"

"Yes."

But I never make the trip. I must not only believe it is a plane, that it will fly, that it is going to California; but there must come a time and point when I make a decision that I will definitely trust that plane and that pilot with my physical life. When I get on the plane, I am depending on the pilot to take me to California. My physical life is in his hands.

That is what it means to believe on Christ. It means I admit that I am a sinner, I believe that I do owe the sin debt like the Bible says, I accept the fact that Jesus Christ has already died and that with His death He paid what I owe as a sinner; and finally it means that I will fully trust Him to get me to Heaven.

Just like I put my physical life in the hands of a pilot to take me across America, so I must put my eternal life in the hands of Jesus to take me to Heaven.

If you can pray this prayer honestly and sincerely, I promise you that when you die you will go to Heaven: "Dear Lord Jesus, I know that I'm a sinner. I do believe You died for me, and here and now I do trust You as my Saviour. From this moment on, I am fully depending on You to get me to Heaven."

If you will trust Him, I promise that you have everlasting life. And you can know that when you die you are going to Heaven.

How can you know it? In John 3:36, Jesus said, "He that believeth on the Son hath everlasting life." God said it. He cannot lie. Hebrews 6:18 says it is impossible for God to lie. If you are trusting Him completely for salvation, you have everlasting life, and you have God's Word for it. If you will write and tell me you have trusted Him, I have some free literature I would like to send you that will help you as you set out to live the Christian life. All you need do to receive your free literature is simply fill out the decision form on the next page and send it to me.

Decision Form

Dr. Shelton Smith
Sword of the Lord
P. O. Box 1099
Murfreesboro, Tennessee 37133-1099
editorial@swordofthelord.com

Dear Dr. Smith:

I have read Dr. Hutson's sermon on Heaven. I do want to go to Heaven when I die. I know that I am a sinner and do believe that Jesus Christ died for me. The best I know how, I trust Him as my Saviour. From this moment on, I am depending on Him to get me to Heaven.

Please pray for me as I set out to live the Christian life.

Date_____

Name_____

Address_____

_____

E-mail_____